For all those who want to learn Japanese seriously and with enthusiasm.

© 2024 Self-taught Japanese

Japan@buchblickverlag.com

Autor:
Hikaru Tamaki
& Andrey Bernhart

Publisher:
Buchblick Verlag
represented by
Andrey Bernhart
Bahnhofstrasse 17
6824 Schlins
Austria

ISBN:
979-8-323-75816-6

Table of contents

Introduction

About the author...Page 6

Romaji & Kana..Page 8

Hiragana & Katakana..Page 9

The 4-step Japanese learning guide.................Page 12

The JLPT N5 Test..Page 16

First recommended video lesson......................Page 18

Quizlet access...Page 19

Learning Hiragana

あ - け...Page 23

   Repetition exercise 1...................................Page 32

   Second video lesson....................................Page 33

こ - つ...Page 34

   Repetition exercise 2 - 3.............................Page 43

   Third video lesson.......................................Page 45

て - ひ...Page 46

    Repetition exercise 4 - 6...................Page 55

ふ - や...Page 58

    Repetition exercise 7 - 9...................Page 67

ゆ - ん...Page 70

    Repetition exercise 10 - 13...............Page 80

3

Learning Katakana

Introduction to Katakana...................Page 86

    Katakana chart...........................Page 87

ア - ケ...Page 88

    Repetition exercise 1.......................Page 97

    Fourth video lesson........................Page 98

コ - ツ...Page 99

    Repetition exercise 2 - 3...................Page 108

テ - ヒ...Page 110

    Repetition exercise 4 - 6...................Page 119

フ - ヤ...Page 122

    Repetition exercise 7 - 10.................Page 131

    Fifth video lesson..........................Page 135

ユ - ン...Page 136

    Repetition exercise 11 - 14...............Page 146

Conclusion

Congratulations!..Page 150

　What's the next step?...................................Page 150

　Dakuon & Handakuon..................................Page 150

　Learn your first 840 words...........................Page 151

Learning with flashcards.................................Page 152

Kana charts..Page 154

　Hiragana..Page 154

　Katakana..Page 155

　Dakuon & Handakuon..................................Page 156

　Yōon..Page 157

Flashcards

Page 158 - 170

1
Introduction

About the author

I conceptualized and wrote this book together with my Japanese teacher. As he wishes to remain anonymous, he uses the pseudonym Hikaru Tamaki. My name is Andrey. I myself grew up in Austria, with German as my mother tongue. Due to my interest in Japanese culture, primarily triggered by anime, manga and Japanese music, one day the thought occurred to me: "Why don't I learn Japanese?"

I was aware that Japanese is one of the most difficult languages for non-native speakers. But that appealed to me even more. I am generally interested in languages and I thought to myself, if I really manage to speak Japanese fluently, any other foreign language will be a piece of cake. True to the motto: if you start with the hardest thing, everything else will be easy afterwards.

Of course, this is meant somewhat humorously, but you really shouldn't underestimate how big and extensive the Japanese language is. For me personally, it is the most beautiful language, but it is also extremely challenging. Especially at the beginning, when you really have no foundation in Japanese at all, it is quite overwhelming for many people. The biggest problem, which I'm sure you've already encountered, is that you can't read the words.

In most of the common foreign languages you learn (I'm talking about French, Spanish, Italian, etc.), at most individual letters are new (we Austrians have ä, ö and ü, for example, which is foreign to most people who don't speak German), but the basic alphabet is the same. We use the Latin or Roman alphabet, which makes it very pleasant to learn foreign languages that use the same or a modified form of our alphabet. Japanese is completely different. Starting with the fact that the Japanese don't just have one alphabet, but three. This means that we first have to learn the alphabet before we can understand even one word of the language. With Spanish or other languages that use the Latin alphabet, we can learn the first words on the first day and perhaps even pronounce the first sentence because we can read the letters. This doesn't work with Japanese.

So there I was, overwhelmed and desperate to learn Japanese, but not knowing where to start. So I watched a few YouTube videos to get some clarity. What struck me immediately was that every Japanese teacher and YouTuber advised me to learn the alphabet first. No sooner said than done, I installed the Kana app (which I would also recommend to you) to practice hiragana and katakana. But since I knew that I would learn faster and more sustainably by writing, I looked around for a writing book to learn Japanese (one like this one).

There were a few on Amazon, but none really met my requirements. So I quickly created one myself. That way, I could make the ideal writing notebook for myself and at the same time I would already be learning the basics of the characters while I was creating the writing notebook. I also got help from Hikaru Tamaki, who helped me to understand the basics of the language and to make the book as effective as possible.

A lot of time has passed since then, and because there was so much interest, I finally published my workbook on Amazon. But only in German at first. After a while, I also translated it into English, where it was an even bigger success than in Germany. You are currently holding the latest and most up-to-date version of it in your hands. I recently wrote a second book in which you learn the 840 vocabulary words for the JLPT N5 (the basic Japanese language test) in 20 weeks.

This workbook was therefore not created from a biased perspective, but by someone who wanted an ideal book for learning. In the meantime, the book has been revised and expanded several times, for example, there are now flashcards at the very end that you can use not only to write, but also to learn. All in all, this writing book is a complete package for learning and perfecting kana, the most important of the 3 writing systems of the Japanese language, from scratch. On the following pages you will find explanations and historical contexts for the most important terms such as kanji, kana, hiragana, katakana, etc. This is followed by my detailed Japanese learning guide, which I worked out myself with the help of Tamaki-san (-san is used formally and means "dear" or actually "honorable Mr/Ms." - that was your first lesson from this book).

Romaji

Before we come to hiragana, it is important to understand romaji. Romaji is the attempt to translate the Japanese alphabet into writing that we can read. In other words, to reproduce the pronunciation of the characters of the Japanese alphabet using letters from our Latin alphabet. This writing system makes it possible for people who are not familiar with Japanese characters to read and pronounce Japanese words.

The hiragana character あ is written in romaji "a". Since we know "a" compared to あ, we can pronounce it. The word hiragana itself, for example, is written in romaij so that we can understand it. In Japanese, hiragana is written like this: ひらがな (ひhiらraがgaなna).

Theoretically, romaji is enough to speak Japanese, so some people skip hiragana and katakana completely and learn vocabulary words based on romaji. For example, they learn that "konnichiwa" means hello, but without being able to read こんにちは (written in hiragana).

Of course, this has many disadvantages. If, like me, you want to read the lyrics of Japanese music, Japanese subtitles in anime or read manga in Japanese, you need to be able to read kana and later also kanji. Music, anime and manga are also a very good way to improve your Japanese once you have mastered the alphabets, basic sentence structure and some vocabulary. You are currently building the foundation for this.

So I strongly recommend not learning with romaji. We use it in this book to help you learn the two basic alphabets. As soon as you have mastered these, however, you should say goodbye to romaji as soon as possible in order to devote yourself fully to the Japanese writing system.

Kana

Together with kanji and romaji, kana is one of the three Japanese writing systems. Kana consists of hiragana and katakana, the two syllabic alphabets of the Japanese language. There are 92 characters in total, 46 per alphabet, which are pronounced the same in both alphabets. In addition, there are modifications called dakuon, handakuon and yōon. Dakuon and handakuon are written diagonally over a hiragana or katakana character and change the pronunciation slightly. For example, か (ka) becomes が (ga) with the dakuon strokes. There are a total of 50 dakuon and handakuon, 25 per alphabet.

Then there are yōon. Yōon are combinations of two hiragana or katakana characters that are pronounced differently than the characters individually. For example, し (shi) and ゆ (yu) becomes しゆ (shu) and not "shiyu". There are 72 of these in total, 36 per alphabet. However, you will also learn these very quickly, as they always have to do with the same three kana characters and also follow very logical rules. Tables for hiragana, katakana, dakuon, handakuon and yōon can be found from page 154 onwards.

However, this explanation is purely so that you have heard of them before. Your focus for this book is clearly on hiragana and katakana. If you can memorize these 92 characters, everything else will be child's play for you. That is why we are now talking about precisely these two alphabets.

Hiragana and katakana

As already mentioned, hiragana and katakana are the two syllable alphabets of the Japanese language. The special feature of a syllable alphabet is that each character consists of either a single vowel (a, e, i, o, u) or a combination of consonant and vowel. Consonants are all other letters that are not vowels.

This means, for example, that "K", "R" or "W" cannot stand alone, but always need a vowel. So instead of "K" there are ka, ki, ku, ke and ko. English words with two or more consonants in a row are therefore very abstract for Japanese to pronounce. The word "three", for example, has a "T", an "H" and an "R" directly after each other, which the Japanese do not know. They would therefore probably pronounce "three" as "teheree", as there are no consonants without a following vowel. This makes it incredibly difficult for Japanese people to learn English pronunciation, whereas it is very easy for us with English (or in my case German) as our mother tongue to pronounce Japanese words.

Another important peculiarity is that the Japanese cannot distinguish between "L" and "R", for them both are the same. The characters ら (ra), り (ri), る (ru), れ (re) and ろ (ro) can therefore also be pronounced la, li, lu, le and lo and, depending on the word, the Japanese are more likely to use "R" or "L".

In addition to hiragana, there is also katakana. Katakana is a syllabary that is identical to hiragana, except that it is used in other situations / for other words than hiragana. It is therefore the same syllables with different characters. While hiragana is the most basic alphabet in the Japanese language, katakana is only used in special situations. For example, foreign words that were originally adopted into Japanese are written using katakana. Pool, for example, would be adopted from English into Japanese and is called プール (pūru) there.

Origin of Hiragana

Hiragana originated in the 9th century as a simplified form of the Chinese characters that were brought to Japan (kanji). Originally there were many variants for each character, but over time the number of characters was standardised. Hiragana was used by Buddhist monks and women at court, as they were denied access to scholarly training in Chinese writing. Hiragana is therefore often referred to as "women's writing", as it was primarily used by women during the Heian period (794-1185).

Today, hiragana is essential for reading and writing in Japanese. It is used together with katakana and kanji to represent the Japanese language in all its facets. Hiragana appears in almost every text, as it is used not only for native Japanese words, but also for grammatical elements that make it possible to understand a sentence. It also facilitates the learning of kanji, as many kanji characters are annotated with hiragana "furigana", small hiragana characters placed next to a kanji to indicate its pronunciation.

Kanji

In addition to romaji and kana, there is a third writing system: Kanji. Kanji are characters that were originally derived from Chinese characters and adopted into the Japanese written language. They represent both whole words and concepts or ideas, and are a central component of the Japanese script. Unlike hiragana and katakana, which are syllabic scripts and each have a specific phonetic value, a kanji can have different pronunciations depending on the context. When learning kanji, a great deal of focus is also placed on the two different readings. Kanji can be read like their original Chinese characters, which is called on'yomi. They can also be read in Japanese, depending on the context, which is called kun'yomi. This diversity makes kanji a particularly complex component of the Japanese writing system.

Despite the large number of kanji in existence - estimates suggest over 50,000 - only around 2,000 to 3,000 characters are needed for everyday use and reading newspapers or books. This collection is known as the "Jōyō Kanji" and includes the characters that the Japanese government considers necessary for everyday use. Schools in Japan teach these characters to ensure that students have mastered the kanji necessary for everyday life in Japan by the end of their compulsory education. An educated Japanese person may well have a repertoire of over 5,000 kanji.

Kanji not only have an important cultural significance in Japan, but also practical advantages. They enable more information to be conveyed with fewer characters, which is particularly useful in the Japanese language, which contains many homophone words (words that sound the same but have different meanings). A single kanji can often represent an entire word or term, which can increase reading speed and make the text more compact.

However, the learning curve for kanji is steep, and mastering these characters requires a lot of practice and memorization. But before you venture into kanji, you should have mastered the basics, which for us are hiragana and katakana.

Stroke order

The stroke order of hiragana characters describes which stroke you start with when writing the characters and how you "swing" them. Unlike our alphabet, the stroke order is strictly defined in Japanese and plays an important role in how the characters are formed. While it doesn't really matter which stroke you draw first for an "H" or "T", for example, it is very important in Japanese.

You can imagine it as a spelling mistake in our language (not 100%, but it's a good metaphor). If you write a colleague's name incorrectly, they won't be happy. It's the same if you write the stroke order incorrectly when writing the name of a Japanese friend. It may seem strange to us, but yes, the Japanese recognize which stroke was written first. You could say they have an eye for it, even if we don't notice it. A wrong stroke order is therefore the same as illegible handwriting and is considered disrespectful.

That's why it's important to learn the stroke order correctly from the start. Remembering the correct stroke order also helps many people to remember the hiragana and katakana characters at the same time.

That's it for the explanations of the most important terms and concepts. Next, I'll present you with a uniform guide to what your learning path in the Japanese language will look like.

The 4-step Japanese learning guide

1. Kana (hiragana & katakana)

As explained earlier, learning the alphabet is by far the most important part of learning a foreign language like Japanese. This is exactly what this writing book is for. At the very end, from page 158 onwards, you will find flashcards on how to memorize kana in other ways in addition to writing exercises.

As soon as you have mastered hiragana and katakana, you should learn dakuon and handakuon. You can do this in a few days once you have mastered hiragana and katakana, as there are very simple rules. More on dakuon and handakuon from page 150, and you will also find some for dakuon and handakuon in the flashcards.

Finally, there are the yōon. Personally, I only really learned these with the 2nd step of the guide, the vocabulary. However, you can use my Quizlet module (see page 19) to practise the yōon in detail if you want to do so before the vocabulary.

2. Learn the 840 N5 words

Next, you should learn vocabulary. Alternatively, many people learn sentence structure, grammar or kanji instead, but I wouldn't advise you to do that. The reason for this is not that it doesn't make sense, but that the fun factor is missing. Many people don't enjoy learning grammar without understanding a single word of the language. Learning kanji also only really makes sense after learning vocabulary, as you come into contact with the first kanji while you are learning vocabulary and learn them passively. This makes it much quicker and easier to learn the kanji later on. Therefore, the second step of the guide is to learn vocabulary. It's best to learn the matching 840 words from the N5 test straight away, then you'll be perfectly prepared. My second book "Your first 840 words in Japanese" deals with exactly these vocabulary words. I would recommend this after this book or alongside it if you want to make rapid progress in your language learning. Of course, I say this because it's my book, but I truly believe it's the fastest and most fun way to learn Japanese sustainably. The sooner and the more vocabulary you know, the more you can really get to grips with the language.

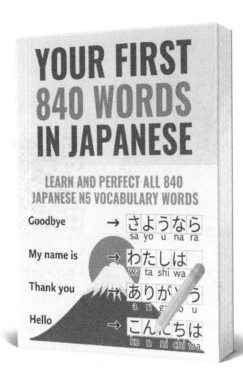

You can go directly to the book on Amazon here

3. Sentence structure and grammar

Now for my personal favorite topic. Once you have mastered all or at least some of the 840 vocabulary words, I recommend learning the basics of Japanese grammar. Japanese grammar is also very logical and (in my opinion) incredibly interesting, which is why I've always enjoyed learning it.

The combination of vocabulary and grammar comprehension also provides the so-called "magic moment " in your learning journey. This is the moment we all started learning Japanese for. Once you have a basic vocabulary and understand the grammar, you suddenly start to understand whole sentences and conversations from Japanese people.

Whether it's anime, manga or Japanese music: you will understand more and more and automatically improve your Japanese just by consuming this media. This is the moment when all that studying really pays off for the first time and the fun begins.

To learn grammar, I recommend my latest and most elaborate book: "Your first 100 sentences in Japanese".

Using the name-giving 100 sentences and over 1,050 Quizlet online exercises,

You can go directly to the book on Amazon here

you will learn the basics of Japanese grammar in the most beginner-friendly and sustainable way possible.

4. Kanji

As a 4th step, I recommend that you learn kanji. For N5 you need about 80 basic kanji, most of which you will learn automatically when you learn vocabulary and grammar.

It also makes sense to learn how to write kanji as early as possible. With this book, you already have a writing book in your hand, which is also available in this form for kanji. I don't (yet) have a kanji writing book myself, as I first want to develop a concept that will enable me to make the best kanji writing book on the English-speaking market. All my books aim to be the best in their category. My Japanese vocabulary book, for example, has always been number 1 of all Japanese vocabulary books on Amazon since it was published. If you are interested in being informed by email when a kanji book is published by us, you can scan the QR code above and enter your email.

The Japanese learning guide

Learn Kana (hiragana and katakana)

These are the two basic alphabets you need to be able to read and write Japanese. That's what this Workbook is for.

Learn your first 840 Japanese Words

The N5 test asks about 800 words and tests your basic vocabulary. You will learn these in my 2nd book.

Learn all the important rules of grammar

Sentence structure, particles, verbs, adjectives and auxiliary verbs. Understanding and forming Japanese sentences. That's what my 3rd book is for: Your first 100 sentences in Japanese

Learn the 80-100 N5 kanji

The third alphabet of the Japanese. Kanji are characters that have independent meanings and appear very frequently in texts.

What is the JLPT N5?

The JLPT (Japanese Language Proficiency Test) N5 is the first and easiest level of the official test to assess your Japanese language proficiency. For many, the goal is to reach N5, N4, N3, N2 and finally N1 (native speaker level). For this, N5 is the first and most important step. Even if your goal is not to reach N1, it makes sense to aim for N5 because you will have a concrete goal to work towards. On the official website, the N5 level is defined as follows: "Understanding simple, typical utterances in everyday situations". You can find a detailed list of what this means here:

Vocabulary and kanji

You should know around 700 - 840 basic words. These words are often used in everyday life, such as "dog" (いぬ), "cat" (ねこ), "eat" (たべる) and "drink" (のむ). You should also learn around 100 basic kanji. Kanji are the Chinese characters used in Japanese, such as 水 (water), 火 (fire) and 人 (person). These words are best learned once you can read basic hiragana and katakana

Grammar

You need to understand the basic rules of Japanese grammar. This means that you should be able to form and understand simple sentences. You should know the most important particles, such as は (wa), が (ga), を (o) and に (ni). These particles will help you to understand the role of the words in the sentence. You also need to master the basic forms of verbs in the present and past tense, as well as their negative forms. For example: "I eat" (たべます) and "I ate" (たべました). Adjectives are also important, both the i-adjectives such as "big" (おおきい) and the na-adjectives such as "calm" (しずか).

Reading comprehension skills

You should be able to read and understand simple texts. These can be short instructions, notes or dialogs. You must also be able to read and write the two syllabic scripts of Japanese, hiragana and katakana, well.

Listening and communication

You need to be able to hold simple conversations and understand everyday situations. This means that you should understand frequently used expressions and simple questions and answers. For example: "How much does that cost?" (これはいくらですか) and "Where is the bathroom?" (トイレはどこですか). This also means that you can introduce yourself and others, make simple greetings and goodbyes and express basic needs and wishes. For example: "I am a student." (わたしはがくせいです) and "I want water." (みずがほしいです).

Writing exercises in this book

On the following pages you will learn a new hiragana character on each page. You will learn kana in columns, which is closest to Japanese writing. Of the total of 9 columns per page, 4 are already easily prescribed so that you simply have to trace the characters there with the pen.

This will help you to draw the characters nicely, especially the first few times. You will notice that Japanese characters are very different to write than our Latin letters with our handwriting.

The remaining 5 columns are empty so that you can practise practising practising practising. It is entirely up to you whether you fill in a page completely the first time or whether you leave columns blank for practicing later.

But don't be too frugal and write as much as possible. There are repetition exercises every 10 pages, where you repeat the last characters you have learned + the characters you have learned previously anyway to internalize them.

Video lessons

At regular intervals, I have linked you to video lessons from well-known personalities that will immerse you further into the world of learning Japanese. Some videos build directly on hiragana and katakana, others have a general focus on helping you learn and learn more about the language in general. Later videos will show you how to pronounce all kana correctly, for example.

You may already be familiar with some of the videos if you have already studied the topic in detail yourself. The video lessons are a bonus and not a must. The main focus of the book is on learning hiragana and katakana, but the videos help you with this and provide a little more context than a simple book could give.

The pages for each video lesson will be structured in the same way. On the left side you will find the QR code to the video and a short description of it. Below or on the right-hand side, you have space for your personal transcript of the video. Some videos also contain a specific question that you can answer here in the book.

First video lesson

QR code to the video:

Scan this QR code to access the first video lesson that I recommend in addition to this book:

The first lesson is from TokuyuuTV, an english speaking Youtube channel that focuses a lot on living in Japan and learning Japanese. It has published what I think is the best beginner video when it comes to this topic. I've already covered most of it in the introduction, but the video is still good for an extra dose of motivation.

For you as a beginner who is just learning hiragana and katakana, the first 3 minutes are especially important. But you can also watch the whole video to find out how he recommends people to learn Japanese

Your notes:

_____

_____

_____

_____

_____

_____

Quizlet access

All 92 kana characters + all 50 dakuon & handakuon + all 66 yōon are now available to learn via my new Quizlet course app!
Quizlet is one of the largest learning platform for teachers and students based on flashcards and is ideal for learning Japanese.

This is how you get access:

Below you will find a QR code or a link. Scan the code or type in the link. Then enter your e-mail address so that your Quizlet access can be sent to you.

If you have already installed the Quizlet app, you will be forwarded directly. If you don't have an account yet, you will find an explanation in the confirmation email of exactly how you need to proceed to get free access to the vocabulary and the Quizlet app:

https://buchblickverlag.com/the-japanese-workbook-quizlet/

ひらがな *Hiragana*

Hiragana chart

	a	i	u	e	o
	あ a	い i	う u	え e	お o
k	か ka	き ki	く ku	け ke	こ ko
s	さ sa	し shi	す su	せ se	そ so
t	た ta	ち chi	つ tsu	て te	と to
n	な na	に ni	ぬ nu	ね ne	の no
h	は ha	ひ hi	ふ fu	へ he	ほ ho
m	ま ma	み mi	む mu	め me	も mo
y	や ya		ゆ yu		よ yo
r	ら ra	り ri	る ru	れ re	ろ ro
w	わ wa				を (w)o
*			ん n		

あ a

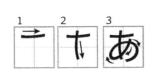

1　2　3

あ

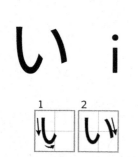

い い

い い

24

う u

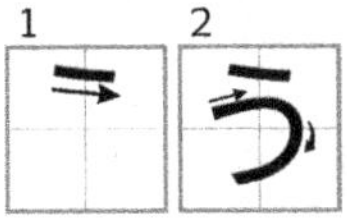

1 → 2 う

う
う
う
う
う
う
う
う
う
う
う
う
う
う
う

う
う
う
う
う
う
う
う
う
う
う
う
う
う
う

う
う
う
う
う
う
う
う
う
う
う
う
う
う
う

う
う
う
う
う
う
う
う
う
う
う
う
う
う
う

え e

え
え
え
え
え
え
え
え
え
え
え
え
え
え

え
え
え
え
え
え
え
え
え
え
え
え
え
え

え
え
え
え
え
え
え
え
え
え
え
え
え
え

え
え
え
え
え
え
え
え
え
え
え
え
え
え
え

お 。

1 2 3
一 お お

お お お お
お お お お
お お お お
お お お お
お お お お
お お お お
お お お お
お お お お
お お お お
お お お お
お お お お
お お お お
お お お お
お お お お

か ka

1	2	3
う	カ	か

か か か か か か
か か か か か か
か か か か か か
か か か か か か
か か か か か か
か か か か か か
か か か か か か
か か か か か か
か か か か か か
か か か か か か
か か か か か か
か か か か か か
か か か か か か
か か か か か か

き ki

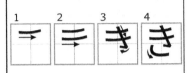

き
き
き
き
き
き
き
き
き
き
き
き
き
き
き
き
き
き
き
き

< ku

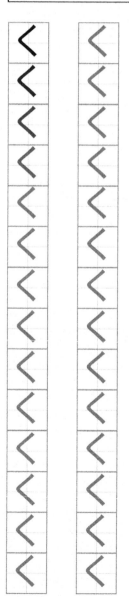

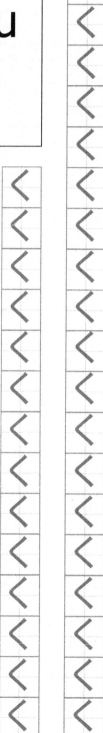

け ke

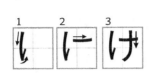

け け

Hiragana repetition exercise 1

a	i	u	e	o	ka	ki	ku	ke
あ	い	う	え	お	か	き	く	け
あ	い	う	え	お	か	き	く	け
あ	い	う	え	お	か	き	く	け
あ	い	う	え	お	か	き		け

Second video lesson

In this second lesson, you will see how all hiragana characters are written and pronounced by a native Japanese. This video will help you get a basic understanding of the writing style as well as the pronunciation.

QR code to the video:

Scan this QR code to access the second video lesson that I recommend in addition to this book:

Your notes:

_____

_____

_____

_____

_____

_____

_____

_____

_____

_____

_____

_____

_____

_____

_____

_____

_____

こ ko

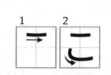

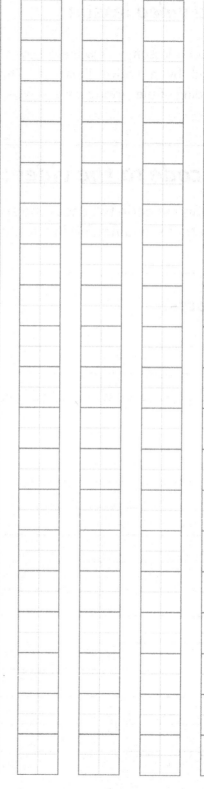

34

さ sa

さ（practice grid characters repeated throughout the page）

し shi

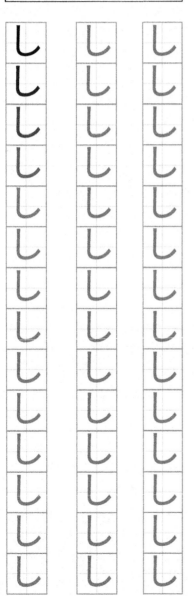

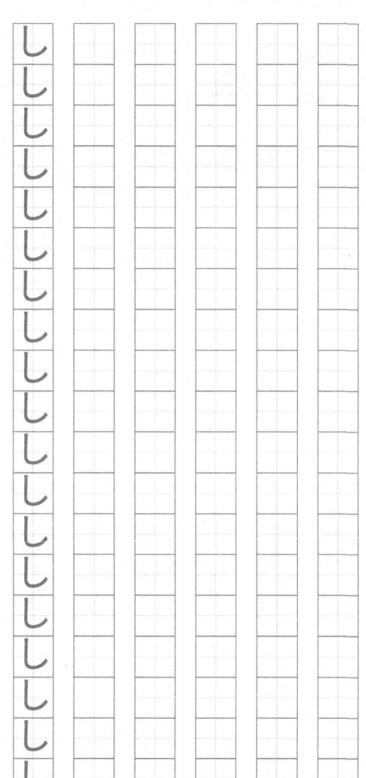

36

す su

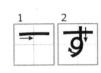

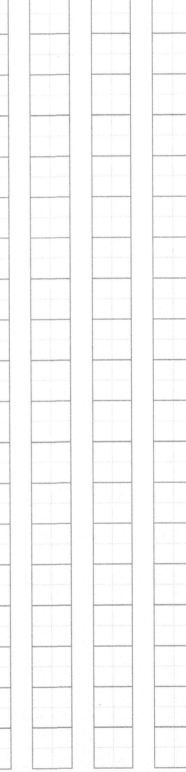

せ se

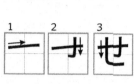

せ せ せ せ

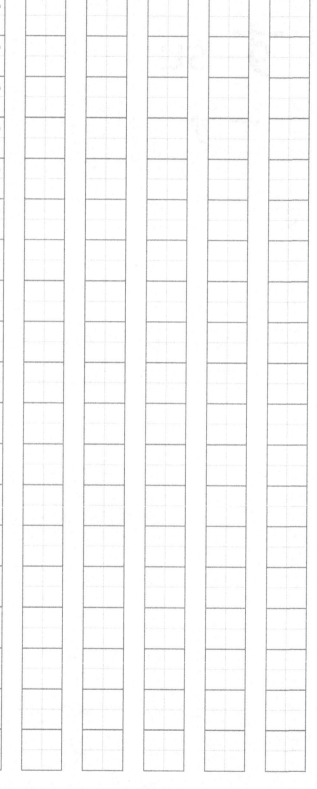

そ SO

そ

そ そ そ そ そ そ

そ そ そ そ そ そ

そ そ そ そ そ そ

そ そ そ そ そ そ

そ そ そ そ そ そ

そ そ そ そ そ そ

そ そ そ そ そ そ

そ そ そ そ そ そ

そ そ そ そ そ そ

そ そ そ そ そ そ

そ そ そ そ そ そ

そ そ そ そ そ そ

そ そ そ そ そ そ

そ そ そ そ そ そ

た　ta

1	2	3	4
⇁	ナ	ナ	た

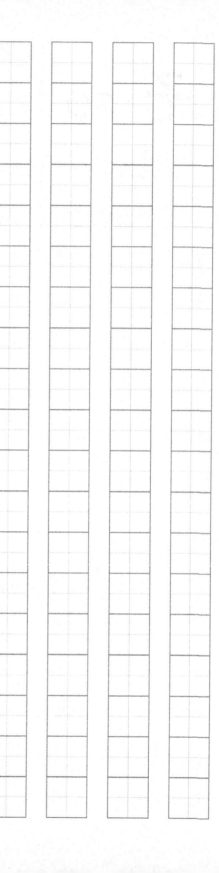

た
た
た
た
た
た
た
た
た
た
た
た
た
た

た
た
た
た
た
た
た
た
た
た
た
た
た
た

た
た
た
た
た
た
た
た
た
た
た
た
た
た

ち chi

ち ち

つ tsu

Hiragana repetition exercise 2

a	i	u	e	o	ka	ki	ku	ke
あ	い	う	え	お	か	き	く	け
あ	い	う	え	お	か	き	く	け
あ	い	う	え	お	か	き	く	け

Hiragana repetition exercise 3

ko	sa	shi	su	se	so	ta	chi	tsu
こ	さ	し	す	せ	そ	た	ち	つ
こ	さ	し	す	せ	そ	た	ち	つ
こ	さ	し	す	せ	そ	た	ち	つ
こ	さ	し	す	せ	そ	た	ち	つ

Third video lesson

The third lesson is from Ruri Ohama, a native Japanese speaker who publishes her videos in English. The video is about the most common mistakes that many people make when learning Japanese. The focus of this lesson is on the attitude you have towards learning Japanese. Answer the question below during or after the video.

QR code to the video:

Scan this QR code to access the third video lesson that I recommend in addition to this book:

Name your 3 reasons for learning Japanese:

_____

_____

_____

_____

_____

Your notes:

_____

_____

_____

_____

_____

_____

_____

て te

て

て て て て
て て て て
て て て て
て て て て
て て て て
て て て て
て て て て
て て て て
て て て て
て て て て
て て て て
て て て て
て て て て
て て て て

と to

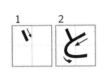

と と と と と と と と と と と と と と と

な　na

1	2	3	4
⇁	ナ	ナ゙	な

な
な
な
な
な
な
な
な
な
な
な
な
な
な
な

な
な
な
な
な
な
な
な
な
な
な
な
な
な
な

な
な
な
な
な
な
な
な
な
な
な
な
な
な
な

な
な
な
な
な
な
な
な
な
な
な
な
な
な
な

に ni

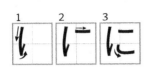

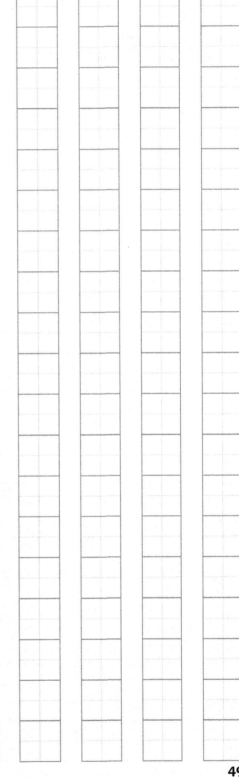

ぬ nu

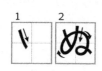

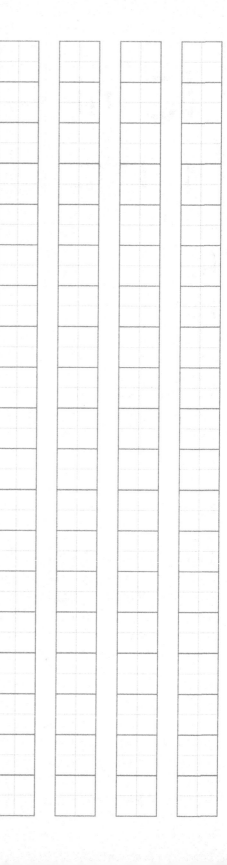

ね ne

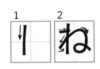

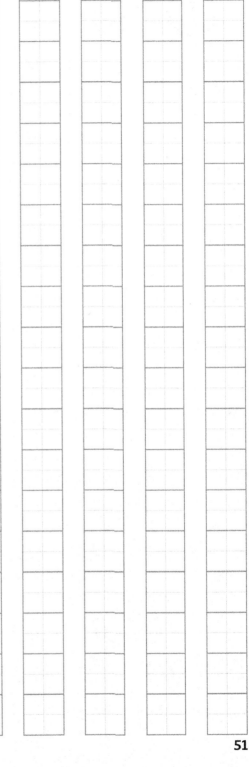

 no

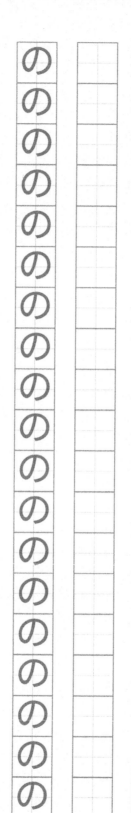

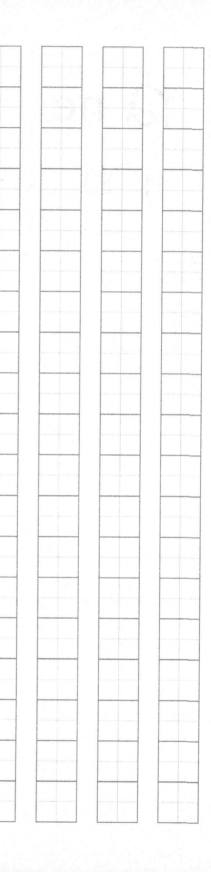

は ha

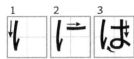

は は は は
は は は は
は は は は
は は は は
は は は は
は は は は
は は は は
は は は は
は は は は
は は は は
は は は は
は は は は
は は は は
は は は は

ひ hi

ひ

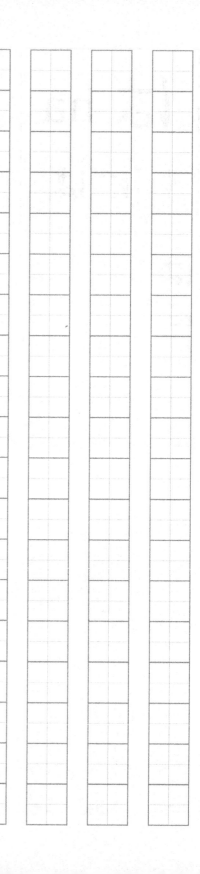

Hiragana repetition exercise 4

a	i	u	e	o	ka	ki	ku	ke
あ	い	う	え	お	か	き	く	け
あ	い	う	え	お	か	き	く	け
あ	い	う	え	お	か	き	く	け

Hiragana repetition exercise 5

ko	sa	shi	su	se	so	ta	chi	tsu
こ	さ	し	す	せ	そ	た	ち	つ
こ	さ	し	す	せ	そ	た	ち	つ
こ	さ	し	す	せ	そ	た	ち	つ
こ	さ	し	す	せ	そ	た	ち	つ

Hiragana repetition exercise 6

te	to	na	ni	nu	ne	no	ha	hi
て	と	な	に	ぬ	ね	の	は	ひ
て	と	な	に	ぬ	ね	の	は	ひ
て	と	な	に	ぬ	ね	の	は	ひ
て	と	な	に	ぬ	ね	の	は	ひ
て								

ふ fu

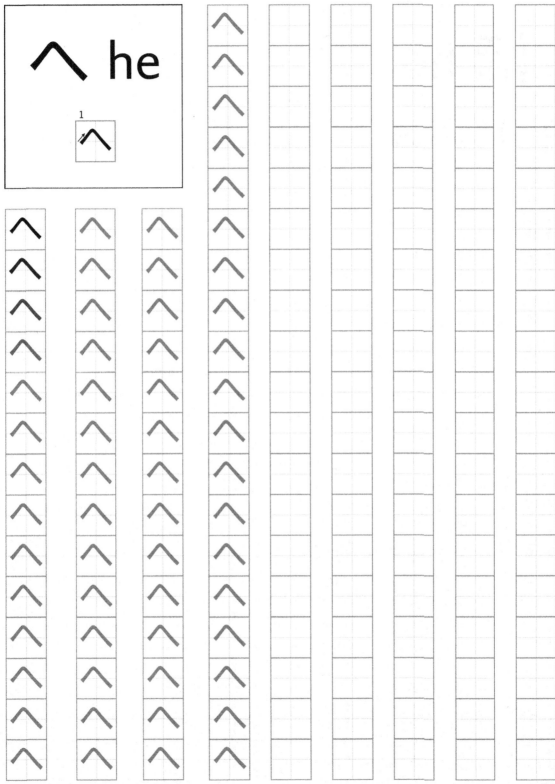

へ he

ほ ho

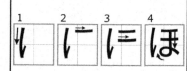

1 2 3 4

ほ ほ ほ

ほ ほ ほ
ほ ほ ほ
ほ ほ ほ
ほ ほ ほ
ほ ほ ほ
ほ ほ ほ
ほ ほ ほ
ほ ほ ほ
ほ ほ ほ
ほ ほ ほ
ほ ほ ほ
ほ ほ ほ
ほ ほ ほ

ま ma

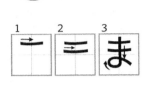

1　2　3

ま

ま ま ま ま
ま ま ま ま
ま ま ま ま
ま ま ま ま
ま ま ま ま
ま ま ま ま
ま ま ま ま
ま ま ま ま
ま ま ま ま
ま ま ま ま
ま ま ま ま
ま ま ま ま
ま ま ま ま

み mi

み
み
み
み
み
み
み
み
み
み
み
み
み
み

み
み
み
み
み
み
み
み
み
み
み
み
み
み

み
み
み
み
み
み
み
み
み
み
み
み
み
み

み
み
み
み
み
み
み
み
み
み
み
み
み
み
み
み

む mu

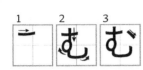

む む む む

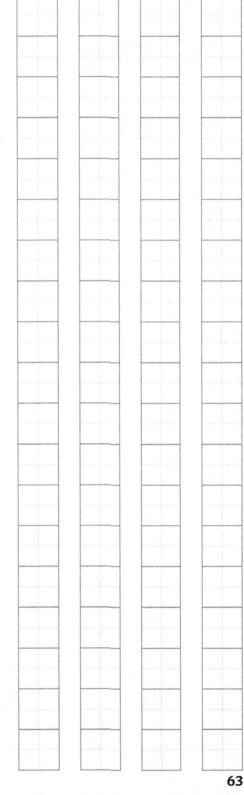

 me

め め め め
め め め め
め め め め
め め め め
め め め め
め め め め
め め め め
め め め め
め め め め
め め め め
め め め め
め め め め
め め め め

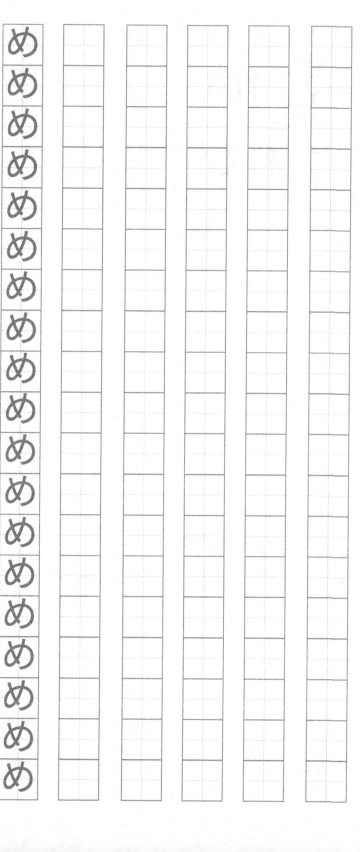

も mo

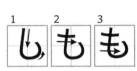

や ya

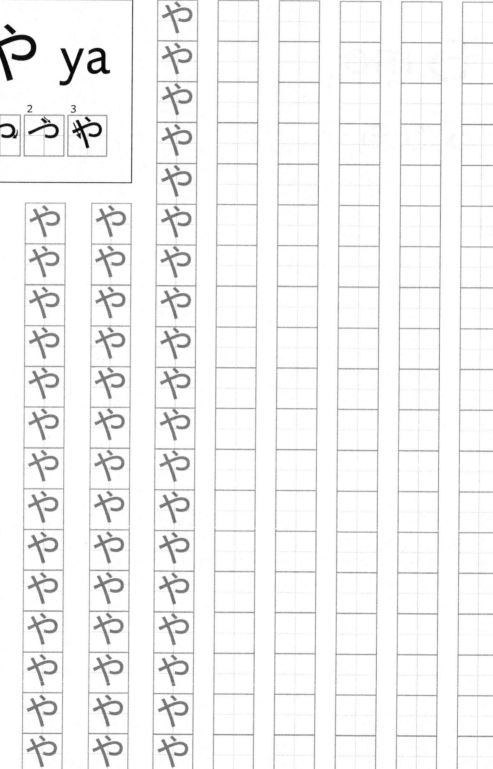

Hiragana repetition exercise 6

ko	sa	shi	su	se	so	ta	chi	tsu
こ	さ	し	す	せ	そ	た	ち	つ
こ	さ	し	す	せ	そ	た	ち	つ
こ	さ	し	す	せ	そ	た	ち	つ
こ	さ	し	す	せ	そ	た	ち	つ

Hiragana repetition exercise 8

te	to	na	ni	nu	ne	no	ha	hi
て	と	な	に	ぬ	ね	の	は	ひ
て	と	な	に	ぬ	ね	の	は	ひ
て	と	な	に	ぬ	ね	の	は	ひ
て	と	な	に	ぬ	ね	の	は	ひ

Hiragana repetition exercise 9

fu	he	ho	ma	mi	mu	me	mo	ya
ふ	へ	ほ	ま	み	む	め	も	や
ふ	へ	に	ま	み	む	め	も	や
ふ	へ	に	ま	み	む	め	も	や
ふ	へ	ほ	ま	み	む	め	も	や
ふ	へ	ほ	ま	み	む	め	も	や

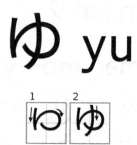

ゆ yu

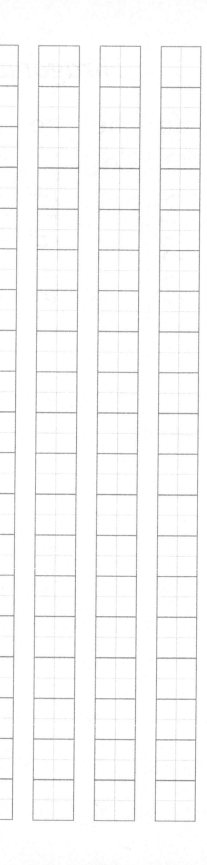

よ yo

よ よ よ よ

ら ra

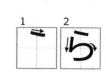

り ri

り

る ru

る

れ re

1 2

れ

ろ ro

ろ

76

わ wa

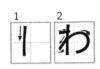

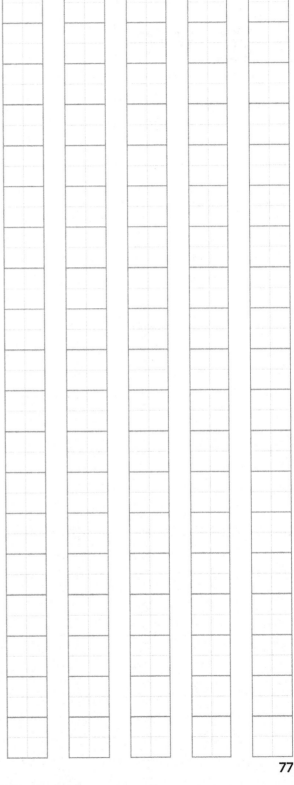

を wo

を
を
を
を
を
を
を
を
を
を
を
を
を
を
を

を
を
を
を
を
を
を
を
を
を
を
を
を
を

を
を
を
を
を
を
を
を
を
を
を
を
を
を

を
を
を
を
を
を
を
を
を
を
を
を
を
を
を

ん n

ん

Hiragana repetition exercise 10

ko	sa	shi	su	se	so	ta	chi	tsu
こ	さ	し	す	せ	そ	た	ち	つ
こ	さ	し	す	せ	そ	た	ち	つ
こ	さ	し	す	せ	そ	た	ち	つ
こ	さ	し	す	せ	そ	た	ち	つ

Hiragana repetition exercise 11

te	to	na	ni	nu	ne	no	ha	hi
て	と	な	に	ぬ	ね	の	は	ひ
て	と	な	に	ぬ	ね	の	は	ひ
て	と	な	に	ぬ	ね	の	は	ひ
て	と	な	に	ぬ	ね	の	は	ひ

Hiragana repetition exercise 12

fu	he	ho	ma	mi	mu	me	mo	ya
ふ	へ	ほ	ま	み	む	め	も	や
ふ	へ	に	ま	み	む	め	も	や
ふ	へ	ほ	ま	み	む	め	も	や
ふ	へ	ほ	ま	み	む	め	も	や
ふ	へ	ほ	ま	み	む	め	も	や

Hiragana repetition exercise 13

yu	yo	ra	ri	ru	re	ro	wa	wo	n
ゆ	よ	ら	り	る	れ	ろ	わ	を	ん
ゆ	よ	ら	り	る	れ	ろ	わ	を	ん
ゆ	よ	ら	り	る	れ	ろ	わ	を	ん
ゆ	よ	ら	り	る	れ	ろ	わ	を	ん
ゆ	よ	ら	り	る	れ	ろ	わ	を	ん

カタカナ

Katakana

Introduction Katakana

Katakana, the second kana alphabet. Like hiragana, it is a syllabary consisting of the same 46 syllables. Here too, each character represents a syllable consisting of a single vowel or a combination of a consonant and a vowel. Hiragana and katakana are basically the same alphabet, but for two different areas of use. While hiragana is the most basic Japanese alphabet, katakana is only used in special cases.

Origin of Katakana

Katakana has its origins in the 9th century and was originally introduced by Buddhist monks. It was created by simplifying parts of Chinese characters, which were used for their phonetic values rather than their meaning. Unlike Hiragana, which was used for native Japanese literature and grammar, Katakana was originally used as an aid for religious texts and scientific terms from Chinese.

Use today

Today, katakana is mainly used for the representation of foreign words, company names, certain scientific and technical terms, names of plants and animals, as well as to emphasize words. An example would be the Japanese word for pool, which was taken from English and is written in katakana プール (pūru). There are many such words in the Japanese language and katakana is mostly used for them.

Another area of application is onomatopoeia (onomatopoeia), which is used in manga and anime. Katakana allows readers to easily distinguish these terms from traditional Japanese words written in hiragana or kanji.

"ドキドキ" (doki doki), for example, occurs frequently in manga and symbolizes a strong palpitating heart. Footsteps, rain, screams, etc. are often written outside the actual speech bubbles in manga with katakana in order to communicate these sounds and convey a certain atmosphere. This is one of many reasons why reading manga in Japanese is a whole new experience compared to the translated version.

Katakana chart

	a	i	u	e	o
	ア a	イ i	ウ u	エ e	オ o
k	カ ka	キ ki	ク ku	ケ ke	コ ko
s	サ sa	シ shi	ス su	セ se	ソ so
t	タ ta	チ chi	ツ tsu	テ te	ト to
n	ナ na	ニ ni	ヌ nu	ネ ne	ノ no
h	ハ ha	ヒ hi	フ fu	ヘ he	ホ ho
m	マ ma	ミ mi	ム mu	メ me	モ mo
y	ヤ ya		ユ yu		ヨ yo
r	ラ ra	リ ri	ル ru	レ re	ロ ro
w	ワ wa				ヲ (w)o
*			ン n		

ア a

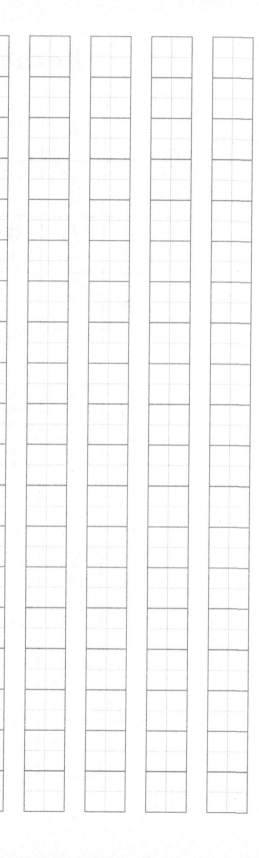

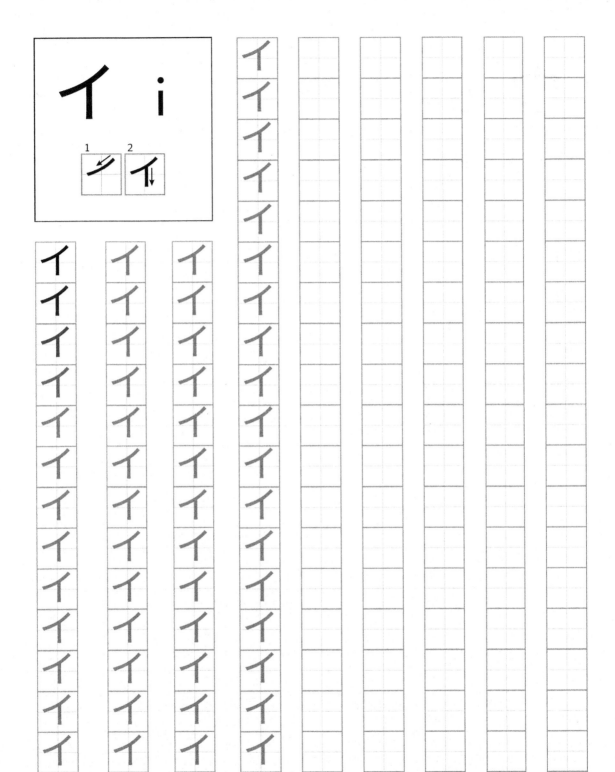

イ i

ウ u

ウ ウ

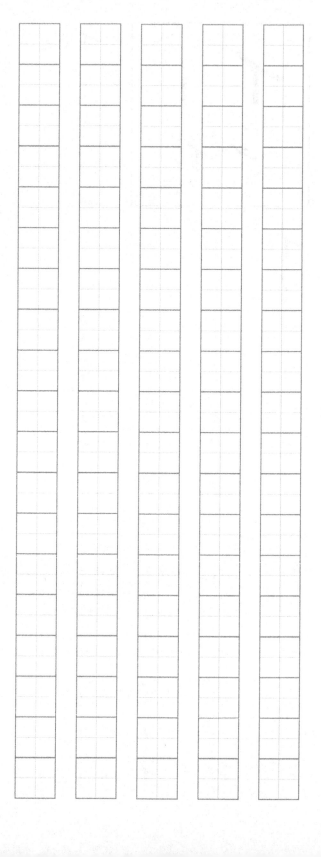

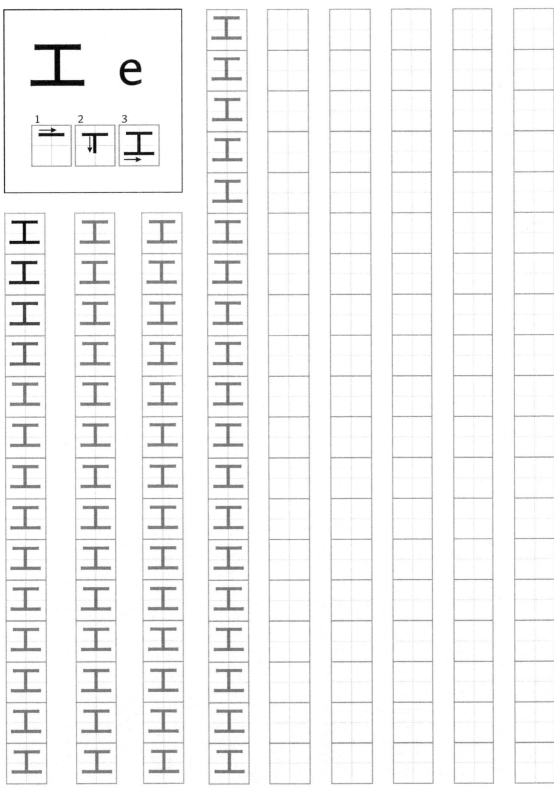

工 e

91

才 。

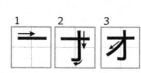

才
才
才
才
才
才
才
才
才
才
才
才
才
才
才
才

才
才
才
才
才
才
才
才
才
才
才
才
才
才
才
才

才
才
才
才
才
才
才
才
才
才
才
才
才
才
才
才

才
才
才
才
才
才
才
才
才
才
才
才
才
才
才
才

カ ka

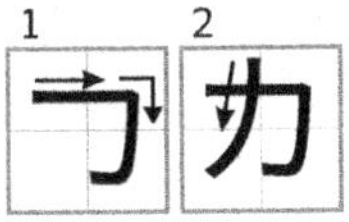

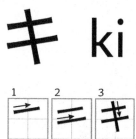 ki

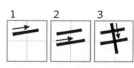

ク ku

ク ク ク ク ク ク ク ク ク ク ク ク ク ク ク

ク ク ク ク ク ク ク ク ク ク ク ク ク ク ク

ク ク ク ク ク ク ク ク ク ク ク ク ク ク ク

ク ク ク ク ク ク ク ク ク ク ク ク ク ク ク

ケ ke

ケ ケ

Katakana repetition exercise 1

a	i	u	e	o	ka	ki	ku	ke
ア	イ	ウ	エ	オ	カ	キ	ク	ケ
ア	イ	ウ	エ	オ	カ	キ	ク	ケ
ア	イ	ウ	エ	オ	カ	キ	ク	ケ
ア	イ	ウ	エ	オ	カ	キ	ク	ケ

Fourth video lesson

In this fourth lesson, you will see how all katakana characters are written and pronounced by a native Japanese. This video will help you get a basic understanding of the writing style of katakana.

QR code to the video:

Scan this QR code to access the fourth video lesson that I recommend in addition to this book:

Your notes:

_____

_____

_____

_____

_____

_____

_____

_____

_____

_____

_____

_____

_____

_____

_____

_____

_____

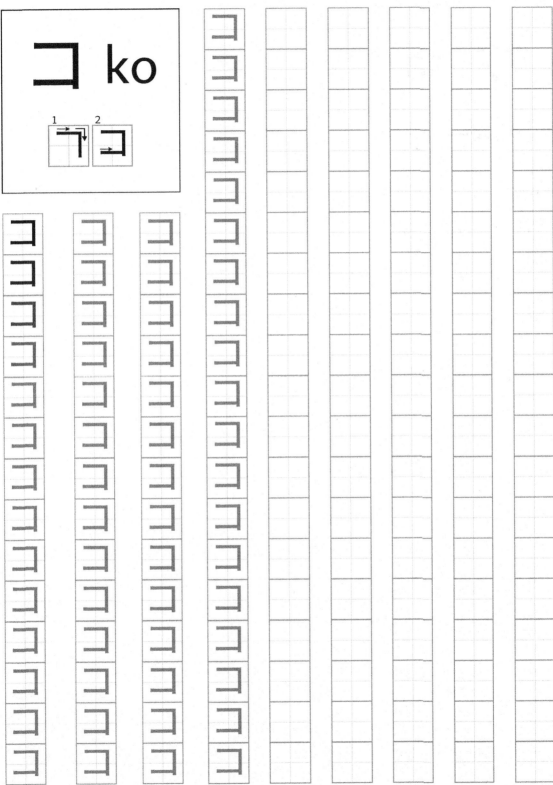

ㄱ ko

サ sa

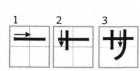

シ shi

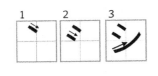

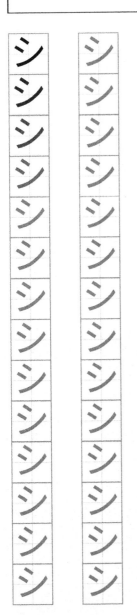

ス su

ス ス ス ス ス ス ス ス ス ス ス

ス ス ス ス ス ス ス ス ス ス ス

ス ス ス ス ス ス ス ス ス ス ス

ス ス ス ス ス ス ス ス ス ス ス ス ス ス ス ス ス

セ se

セ
セ
セ
セ
セ
セ
セ
セ
セ
セ
セ
セ
セ
セ

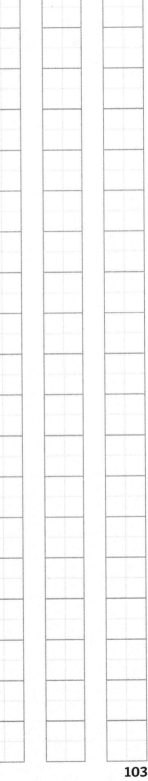

ソ **SO**

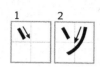

ソ ソ ソ ソ ソ ソ

104

タ ta

1	2	3
ノ	ク	タ

タ タ タ タ タ タ タ タ タ タ タ タ タ タ タ

タ タ タ タ タ タ タ タ タ タ タ タ タ タ タ

タ タ タ タ タ タ タ タ タ タ タ タ タ タ タ

タ タ タ タ タ タ タ タ タ タ タ タ タ タ タ

チ chi

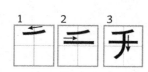

チ チ チ チ チ チ チ チ チ チ チ チ チ チ チ

チ チ チ チ チ チ チ チ チ チ チ チ チ チ チ

チ チ チ チ チ チ チ チ チ チ チ チ チ チ チ

チ チ チ チ チ チ チ チ チ チ チ チ チ チ チ

ツ tsu

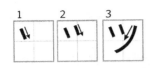

ツ ツ ツ ツ ツ ツ ツ ツ ツ ツ ツ ツ ツ ツ

ツ ツ ツ ツ ツ ツ ツ ツ ツ ツ ツ ツ ツ ツ

ツ ツ ツ ツ ツ ツ ツ ツ ツ ツ ツ ツ ツ ツ

ツ ツ ツ ツ ツ ツ ツ ツ ツ ツ ツ ツ ツ ツ

Katakana repetition exercise 2

a	i	u	e	o	ka	ki	ku	ke
ア	イ	ウ	エ	オ	カ	キ	ク	ケ
ア	イ	ウ	エ	オ	カ	キ	ク	ケ
ア	イ	ウ	エ	オ	カ	キ	ク	ケ
ア	イ	ウ	エ	オ	カ	キ	ク	ケ

Katakana repetition exercise 3

ko	sa	shi	su	se	so	ta	chi	tsu
コ	サ	シ	ス	セ	ソ	タ	チ	ツ
コ	サ	シ	ス	セ	ソ	タ	チ	ツ
コ	サ	シ	ス	セ	ソ	タ	チ	ツ
コ	サ	シ	ス	セ	ソ	タ	チ	ツ

テ te

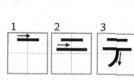

テ
テ
テ
テ
テ
テ
テ
テ
テ
テ
テ
テ

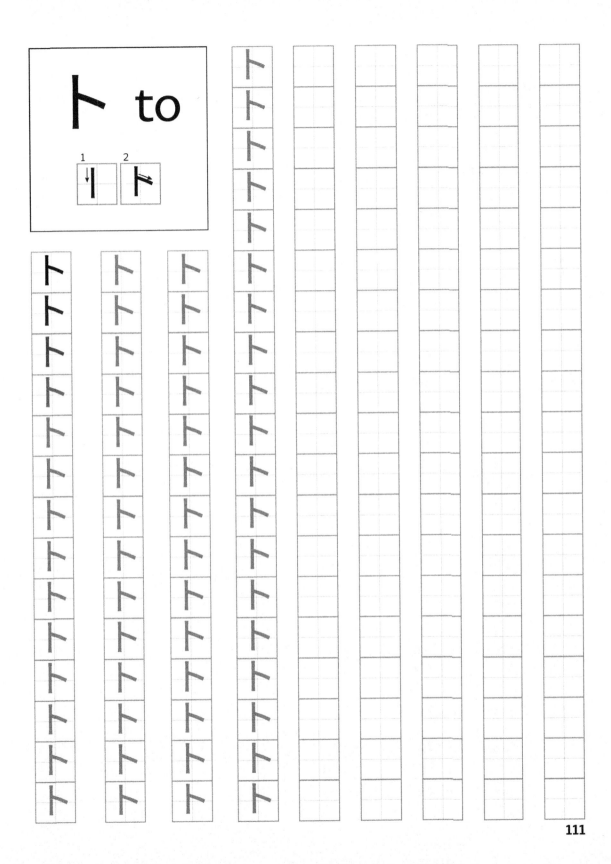

ト　to

111

ナ na

ナ
ナ
ナ
ナ
ナ
ナ
ナ
ナ
ナ
ナ
ナ
ナ
ナ
ナ
ナ

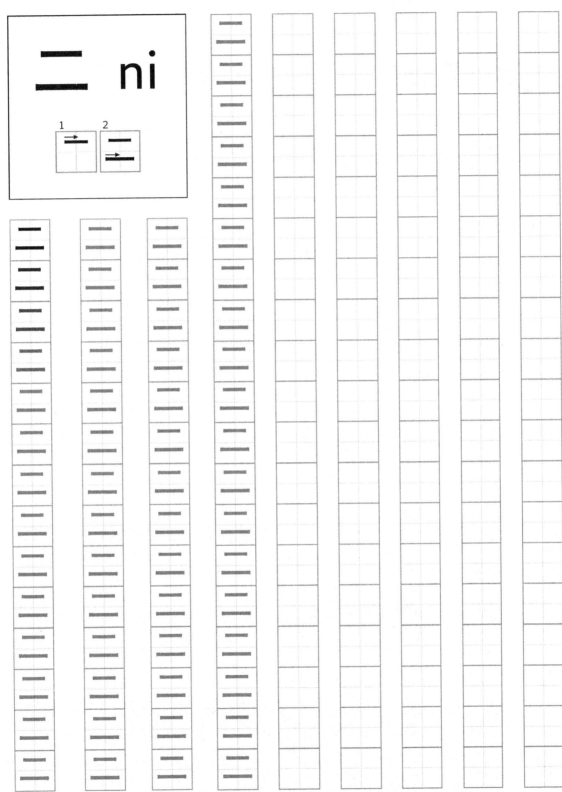

ヌ nu

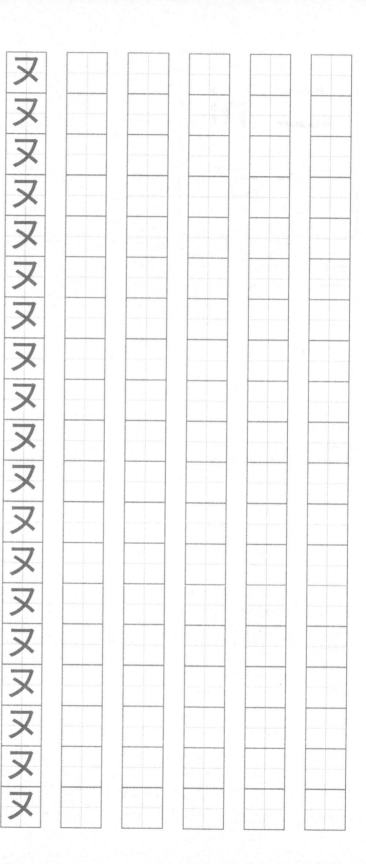

ヌ ヌ ヌ ヌ

ネ ne

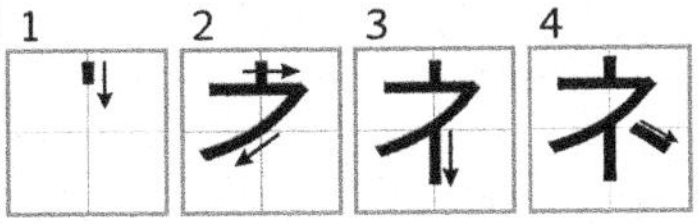

1	2	3	4
	ナ	ネ	ネ

ネ
ネ
ネ
ネ
ネ
ネ
ネ
ネ
ネ
ネ
ネ
ネ

ネ
ネ
ネ
ネ
ネ
ネ
ネ
ネ
ネ
ネ
ネ
ネ

ネ
ネ
ネ
ネ
ネ
ネ
ネ
ネ
ネ
ネ
ネ
ネ

ネ
ネ
ネ
ネ
ネ
ネ
ネ
ネ
ネ
ネ
ネ
ネ
ネ
ネ

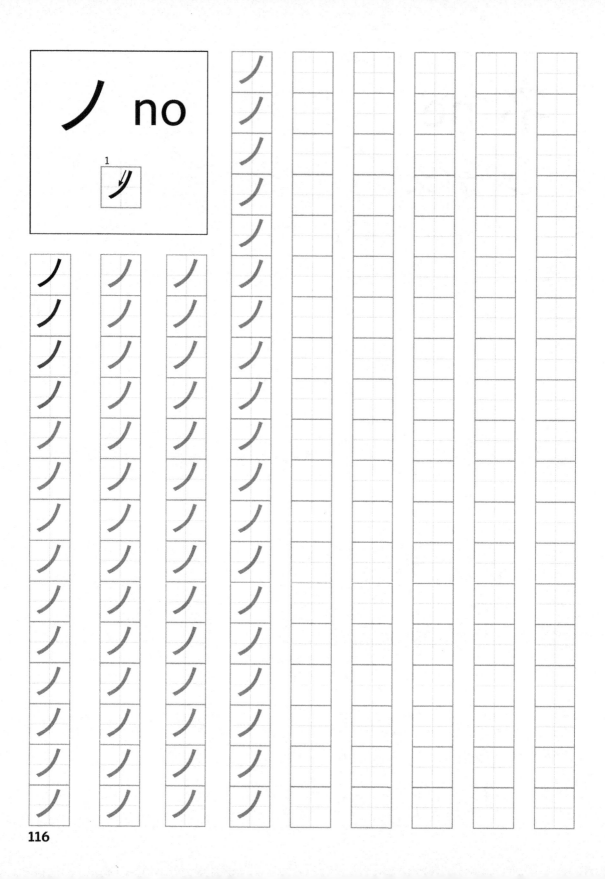

ノ no

ハ ha

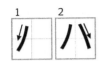

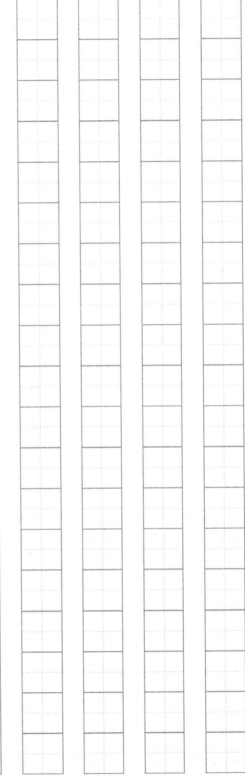

ヒ hi

ヒ ヒ ヒ ヒ ヒ ヒ
ヒ ヒ ヒ ヒ
ヒ ヒ ヒ ヒ
ヒ ヒ ヒ ヒ
ヒ ヒ ヒ ヒ
ヒ ヒ ヒ ヒ
ヒ ヒ ヒ ヒ
ヒ ヒ ヒ ヒ
ヒ ヒ ヒ ヒ
ヒ ヒ ヒ ヒ
ヒ ヒ ヒ ヒ
ヒ ヒ ヒ ヒ
ヒ ヒ ヒ ヒ
ヒ ヒ ヒ ヒ
ヒ ヒ ヒ ヒ

Katakana repetition exercise 4

a	i	u	e	o	ka	ki	ku	ke
ア	イ	ウ	エ	オ	カ	キ	ク	ケ
ア	イ	ウ	エ	オ	カ	キ	ク	ケ
ア	イ	ウ	エ	オ	カ	キ	ク	ケ
ア	イ	ウ	エ	オ	カ	キ	ク	ケ

Katakana repetition exercise 5

ko	sa	shi	su	se	so	ta	chi	tsu
コ	サ	シ	ス	セ	ソ	タ	チ	ツ
コ	サ	シ	ス	セ	ソ	ク	ニ	ツ
コ	サ	シ	ス	セ	ソ	タ	チ	ツ
コ	サ	シ	ス	セ	ソ	タ	チ	ツ
コ	サ	シ	ス	セ	ソ	タ	チ	ツ

Katakana repetition exercise 6

te	to	na	ni	nu	ne	no	ha	hi
テ	ト	ナ	ニ	ヌ	ネ	ノ	ハ	ヒ
テ	ト	ナ	ニ	ヌ	ネ	ノ	ハ	ヒ
テ	ト	ナ	ニ	ヌ	ネ	ノ	ハ	ヒ
テ	ト	ナ	ニ	ヌ	ネ	ノ	ハ	ヒ
テ	ト	ナ	ニ	ヌ	ネ	ノ	ハ	ヒ

フ fu

フ

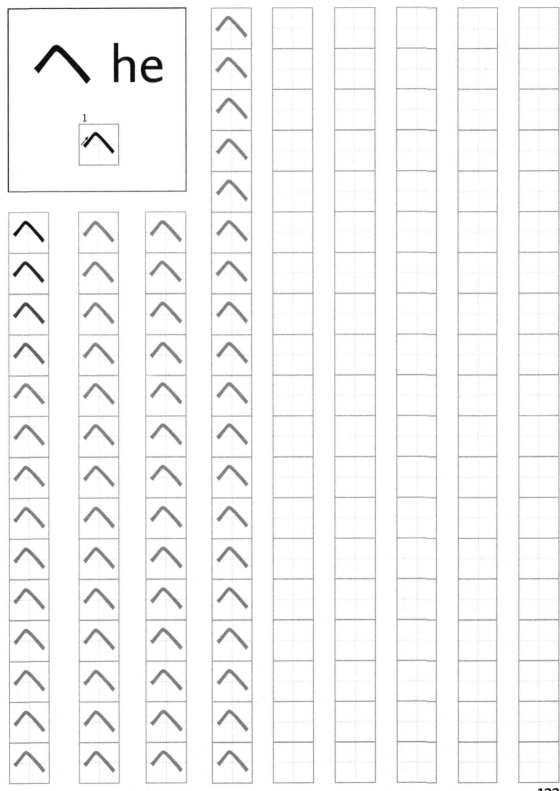

へ he

ホ ho

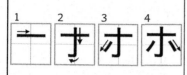

ホ ホ ホ ホ
ホ ホ ホ ホ
ホ ホ ホ ホ
ホ ホ ホ ホ
ホ ホ ホ ホ
ホ ホ ホ ホ
ホ ホ ホ ホ
ホ ホ ホ ホ
ホ ホ ホ ホ
ホ ホ ホ ホ
ホ ホ ホ ホ
ホ ホ ホ ホ
ホ ホ ホ ホ
ホ ホ ホ ホ
ホ ホ ホ ホ
ホ ホ ホ ホ

 ma

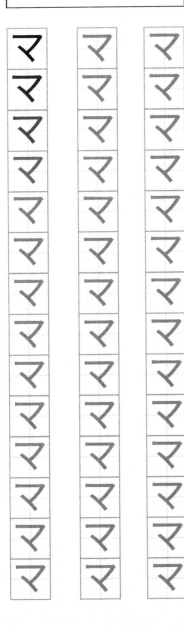

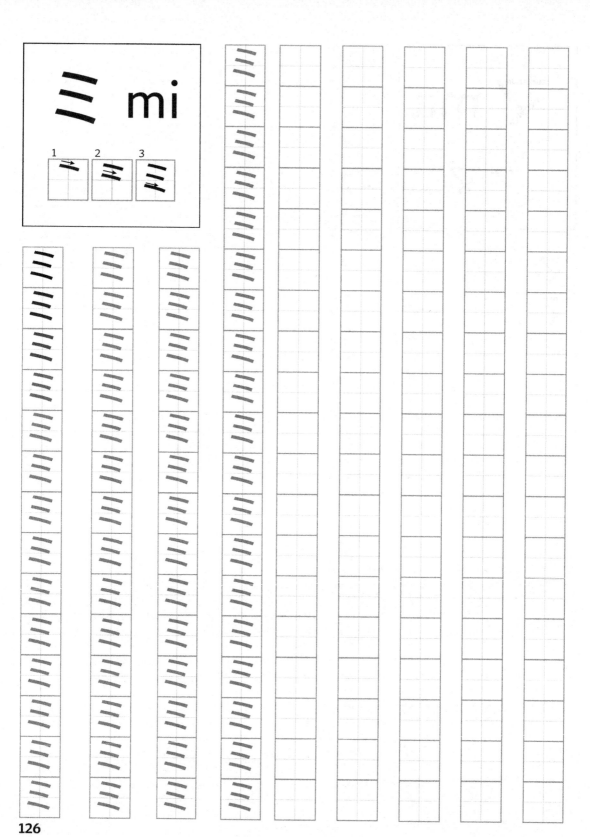

三 mi

126

Ʌ mu

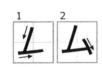

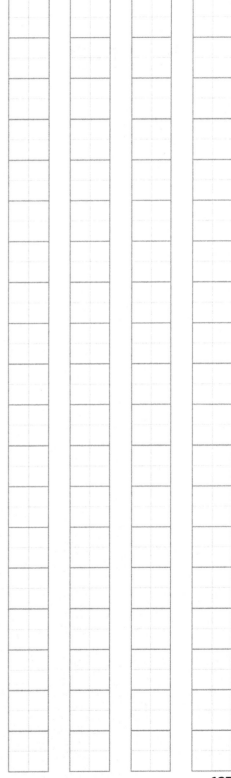

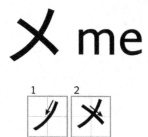 me

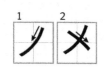

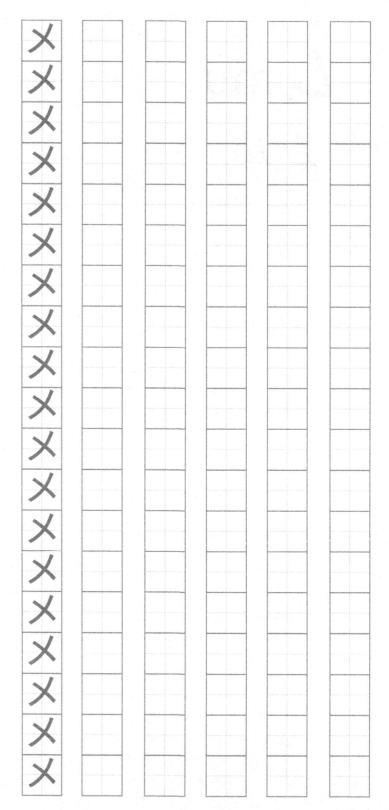

128

毛 mo

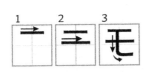

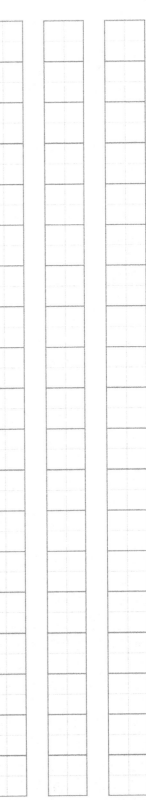

ㄚ ya

130

Katakana repetition exercise 7

a	i	u	e	o	ka	ki	ku	ke
ア	イ	ウ	エ	オ	カ	キ	ク	ケ
ア	イ	ウ	エ	オ	カ	キ	ク	ケ
ア	イ	ウ	エ	オ	カ	キ	ク	ケ
ア	イ	ウ	エ	オ	カ	キ	ク	ケ

Katakana repetition exercise 8

ko	sa	shi	su	se	so	ta	chi	tsu
コ	サ	シ	ス	セ	ソ	タ	チ	ツ
コ	サ	シ	ス	セ	ソ	タ	チ	ツ
コ	サ	シ	ス	セ	ソ	タ	チ	ツ
コ	サ	シ	ス	セ	ソ	タ	チ	ツ

Katakana repetition exercise 9

te	to	na	ni	nu	ne	no	ha	hi
テ	ト	ナ	ニ	ヌ	ネ	ノ	ハ	ヒ
テ	ト	ナ	ニ	ヌ	ネ	ノ	ハ	ヒ
テ	ト	ナ	ニ	ヌ	ネ	ノ	ハ	ヒ
テ	ト	ナ	ニ	ヌ	ネ	ノ	ハ	ヒ

Katakana repetition exercise 10

fu	he	ho	ma	mi	mu	me	mo	ya
フ	ヘ	一	ブ	ニ	ム	ノ	二	ヤ
フ	ヘ	ナ	マ	ミ	ム	メ	モ	ヤ
フ	ヘ	オ	マ	ミ	ム	メ	モ	ヤ
フ	ヘ	ホ	マ	ミ	ム	メ	モ	ヤ
フ	ヘ	ホ	マ	ミ	ム	メ	モ	ヤ

Fifth video lesson

In this fifth lesson, you will learn the basics of Japanese pronunciation. There are many peculiarities and special features of pronunciation in the Japanese language, and this video helped me to understand the language better, especially at the beginning.

QR code to the video:

Scan this QR code to access the fifth video lesson that I recommend in addition to this book:

Your notes:

_____

_____

_____

_____

_____

_____

_____

_____

_____

_____

_____

_____

_____

_____

_____

_____

_____

ユ yu

ユ ユ ユ ユ ユ ユ ユ ユ ユ ユ ユ ユ ユ ユ ユ

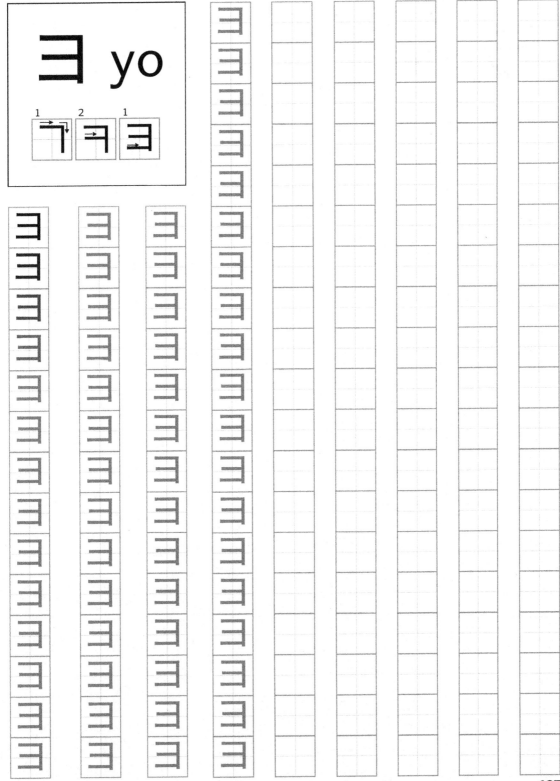

ヨ yo

ラ ra

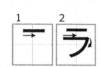

ラ ラ ラ ラ ラ ラ ラ ラ ラ ラ ラ ラ ラ ラ ラ ラ

リ ri

リ

ル ru

ル ル ル ル

ル ル ル ル
ル ル ル ル
ル ル ル ル
ル ル ル ル
ル ル ル ル
ル ル ル ル
ル ル ル ル
ル ル ル ル
ル ル ル ル
ル ル ル ル
ル ル ル ル
ル ル ル ル
ル ル ル ル
ル ル ル ル

レ re

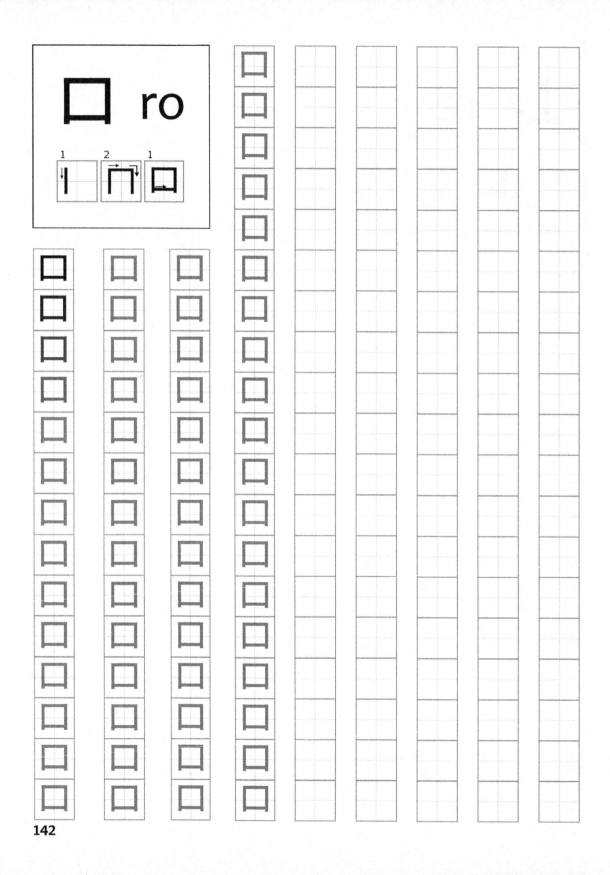

ro

ワ wa

ワ ワ

ヲ WO

ヲ ヲ ヲ ヲ ヲ ヲ ヲ ヲ ヲ ヲ ヲ ヲ ヲ ヲ ヲ ヲ ヲ ヲ ヲ

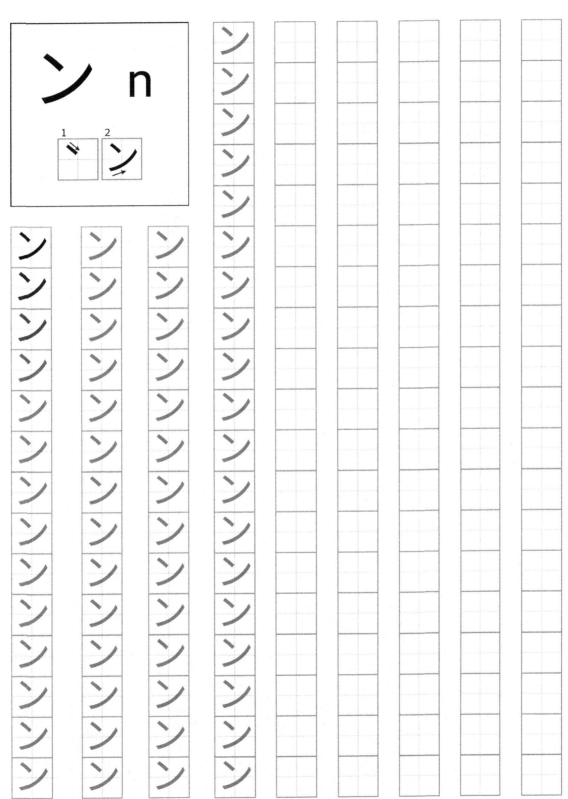

Katakana repetition exercise 11

ko	sa	shi	su	se	so	ta	chi	tsu
コ	サ	シ	ス	セ	ソ	タ	チ	ツ
コ	サ	シ	ス	セ	ソ	タ	チ	ツ
コ	サ	シ	ス	セ	ソ	タ	チ	ツ
コ	サ	シ	ス	セ	ソ	タ	チ	ツ

Katakana repetition exercise 12

te	to	na	ni	nu	ne	no	ha	hi
テ	ト	ナ	ニ	ヌ	ネ	ノ	ハ	ヒ
テ	ト	ナ	ニ	ヌ	ネ	ノ	ハ	ヒ
テ	ト	ナ	ニ	ヌ	ネ	ノ	ハ	ヒ
テ	ト	ナ	ニ	ヌ	ネ	ノ	ハ	ヒ
テ	ト	ナ	ニ	ヌ	ネ	ノ	ハ	ヒ

147

Katakana repetition exercise 13

fu	he	ho	ma	mi	mu	me	mo	ya
フ	ヘ	ホ	マ	ミ	ム	メ	モ	ヤ
フ	ヘ	ナ	マ	ミ	ム	メ	ニ	ヤ
フ	ヘ	オ	マ	ミ	ム	メ	モ	ヤ
フ	ヘ	ホ	マ	ミ	ム	メ	モ	ヤ
フ	ヘ	ホ	マ	ミ	ム	メ	モ	ヤ

Katakana repetition exercise 14

yu	yo	ra	ri	ru	re	ro	wa	wo	n
ユ	ヨ	ラ	リ	ル	レ	ロ	ワ	ヲ	ン
ユ	ヨ	ラ	リ	ル	レ	ロ	ワ	ヲ	ン
ユ	ヨ	ラ	リ	ル	レ	ロ	ワ	ヲ	ン
ユ	ヨ	ラ	リ	ル	レ	ロ	ワ	ヲ	ン

Congratulations!

Congratulations! You have reached the end of this book and should now have a solid foundation in hiragana and katakana. If you are not yet able to memorize all of the 92 characters, this is completely normal. Repeat the characters over and over again and keep practicing diligently. That's exactly why I've added the flashcards to the last pages of the book, so that you can continue learning with them. At some point, it will become quite intuitive for you to read the signs. You will probably already have some signs that are absolutely logical and recognizable to you within milliseconds.

What's the next step?

You can complete Kana next. After that, you'll be more than ready to learn your first 840 words and finally understand your first Japanese sentences. To fully master kana, you still need dakuon, handakuon and yōon. The most effective way to learn yōon is with the Kana app or in parallel with vocabulary learning (that's how I did it). The dakuon and handakuon can best be learned here in this book.

Dakuon﹅ and Handakuon˚

Dakuon and handakuon are small characters in Japanese writing that are added to hiragana and katakana to change the pronunciation of the basic characters. Dakuon and handakuon are types of modified consonant sounds in Japanese kana. Dakuon are voiced sounds created by adding a small diacritic mark called "dakuten" (﹅) to certain kana, for example, か (ka) becomes が (ga) and さ (sa) becomes ざ (za), while handakuon are semi-voiced sounds created by adding a small circle called "handakuten" (˚) to certain kana, specifically the "h" row, for example, は (ha) becomes ぱ (pa), these modifications change the pronunciation of the kana, adding richness and variety to the Japanese phonetic system.
Now that you know hiragana and katakana, it is not difficult to learn dakuon and handakuon. Look at the chart for both a few pages further on and study for 2 - 3 days with the dakuon and handakuon flashcards from this book, that should be enough for you to memorize them.

Your first 840 Japanese words

Your next big challenge is called N5. You now know hiragana and katakana, the hardest step and therefore the foundation has been completed, the next task is to learn your first 840 Japanese words.

To make this task as easy and exciting as possible, I have written a second book: "Your first 840 Japanese words". Using the ingenious flashcard strategy, you will learn 42 new Japanese words every week. So after just 20 weeks you will know all 840 N5 words!

For me personally, however, it was never about the N5 test, but about what I could do with the words. Of course, it's important to have a goal and N5 as an initial goal is very reasonable. But it was much better to finally be able to understand many Japanese words and even sentences with the 840 vocabulary words. I finally understood individual statements from anime or could understand the lyrics of Japanese songs. It's an indescribable sense of achievement to finally be able to understand parts of this complex language. If you're ready for the next step in your journey, learn your first 840 words in Japanese and order my second book now on Amazon. Just search "Your first 840 Japanese words" or scan the QR code:

You can go directly to the book on Amazon here

Learning with flashcards

On the following pages you will find all 92 hiragana and katakana characters + all 50 dakuon and handakuon as flashcards to cut out. You can practice with them every day to help you remember them even better. One side is deliberately printed upside down so that you can turn the cards upside down and don't have to turn them sideways. You'll understand what I mean as soon as you hold them in your hands.

If you have enjoyed the book so far, and it has helped you, I would like to ask you a favor at the end. Please take 2 - 3 minutes and rate the book here on Amazon with your honest opinion. This would really support me the most and help me to publish more books like this in the future. Just go to your orders on Amazon, or scan the QR code here.

Finally, I would just like to say thank you for taking the time to work through my book. It is truly an honor to be a support to you on your journey of learning Japanese. I wish you all the best, much success and, above all, lots of fun learning this fascinating language!

A. B.

Hiragana chart

	a	i	u	e	o
	あ a	い i	う u	え e	お o
k	か ka	き ki	く ku	け ke	こ ko
s	さ sa	し shi	す su	せ se	そ so
t	た ta	ち chi	つ tsu	て te	と to
n	な na	に ni	ぬ nu	ね ne	の no
h	は ha	ひ hi	ふ fu	へ he	ほ ho
m	ま ma	み mi	む mu	め me	も mo
y	や ya		ゆ yu		よ yo
r	ら ra	り ri	る ru	れ re	ろ ro
w	わ wa				を (w)o
*			ん n		

Katakana chart

	a	i	u	e	o
	ア a	イ i	ウ u	エ e	オ o
k	カ ka	キ ki	ク ku	ケ ke	コ ko
s	サ sa	シ shi	ス su	セ se	ソ so
t	タ ta	チ chi	ツ tsu	テ te	ト to
n	ナ na	ニ ni	ヌ nu	ネ ne	ノ no
h	ハ ha	ヒ hi	フ fu	ヘ he	ホ ho
m	マ ma	ミ mi	ム mu	メ me	モ mo
y	ヤ ya		ユ yu		ヨ yo
r	ラ ra	リ ri	ル ru	レ re	ロ ro
w	ワ wa				ヲ (w)o
*			ン n		

Dakuon & Handakuon chart

	a	i	u	e	o
g	が ga	ぎ gi	ぐ gu	げ ge	ご go
z	ざ za	じ ji	ず zu	ぜ ze	ぞ zo
d	だ da	ぢ ji (di)	づ zu (du)	で de	ど do
b	ば ba	び bi	ぶ bu	べ be	ぼ bo
p	ぱ pa	ぴ pi	ぷ pu	ぺ pe	ぽ po

	a	i	u	e	o
g	ガ ga	ギ gi	グ gu	ゲ ge	ゴ go
z	ザ za	ジ ji	ズ zu	ゼ ze	ゾ zo
d	ダ da	ヂ ji (di)	ヅ zu (du)	デ de	ド do
b	バ ba	ビ bi	ブ bu	ベ be	ボ bo
p	パ pa	ピ pi	プ pu	ペ pe	ポ po

Yōon chart

	Hiragana			Katakana		
	や	ゆ	よ	ヤ	ユ	ヨ
ky	きゃ kya	きゅ kyu	きょ kyo	キャ kya	キュ kyu	キョ kyo
gy	ぎゃ gya	ぎゅ gyu	ぎょ gyo	ギャ gya	ギュ gyu	ギョ gyo
sh	しゃ sha	しゅ shu	しょ sho	シャ sha	シュ shu	ショ sho
j	じゃ ja	じゅ ju	じょ jo	ジャ ja	ジュ ju	ジョ jo
ch	ちゃ cha	ちゅ chu	ちょ cho	チャ cha	チュ chu	チョ cho
j	ぢゃ ja	ぢゅ ju	ぢょ jo	ヂャ ja	ヂュ ju	ヂョ jo
ny	にゃ nya	にゅ nyu	にょ nyo	ニャ nya	ニュ nyu	ニョ nyo
hy	ひゃ hya	ひゅ hyu	ひょ hyo	ヒャ hya	ヒュ hyu	ヒョ hyo
by	びゃ bya	びゅ byu	びょ byo	ビャ bya	ビュ byu	ビョ byo
py	ぴゃ pya	ぴゅ pyu	ぴょ pyo	ピャ pya	ピュ pyu	ピョ pyo
my	みゃ mya	みゅ myu	みょ myo	ミャ mya	ミュ myu	ミョ myo
ry	りゃ rya	りゅ ryu	りょ ryo	リャ rya	リュ ryu	リョ ryo

Hiragana flashcards

あ	い	う	え
お	か	き	く
け	こ	さ	し
す	せ	そ	た
ち	つ	て	と
な	に	ぬ	ね

e	u	i	a
ku	ki	ka	o
shi	sa	ko	ke
ta	so	se	su
to	te	tsu	chi
ne	nu	ni	na

の	は	ひ	ふ
へ	ほ	ま	み
む	め	も	や
ゆ	よ	ら	り
る	れ	ろ	わ
を	ん	*For reasons of space, here is the first Dakuon flashcard* →	が

wo	n	*For reasons of space, here is the first Dakuon flashcard* →	ga
ru	re	ro	wa
yu	yo	ra	ri
mu	me	mo	ya
he	ho	ma	mi
ou	ha	hi	fu

ア	イ	ウ	エ
オ	カ	キ	ク
ケ	コ	サ	シ
ス	セ	ソ	タ
チ	ツ	テ	ト
ナ	ニ	ヌ	ネ

e	u	i	a
ku	ki	ka	o
shi	sa	ko	ke
ta	so	se	su
to	te	tsu	chi
ne	nu	ni	na

Katakana flashcards

ノ	ハ	ヒ	フ
ヘ	ホ	マ	ミ
ム	メ	モ	ヤ
ユ	ヨ	ラ	リ
ル	レ	ロ	ワ
ヲ	ン	*For reasons of space, here is the first Dakuon flashcard* ↘	ガ

wo	n	*For reasons of space, here is the first Dakuon flashcard* ⟶	ga
ru	re	ro	wa
yu	yo	ra	ri
mu	me	mo	ya
he	ho	ma	mi
ou	ha	hi	fu

ぎ	ぐ	げ	ご
ざ	じ	ず	ぜ
ぞ	だ	ぢ	づ
で	ど	ば	び
ぶ	べ	ぼ	ぱ
ぴ	ぷ	ぺ	ぽ

oɓ	əɓ	nɓ	iɓ
əz	nz	ji	ɐz
np	ip	ɐp	oz
iq	ɐq	op	əp
ɐd	oq	əq	nq
od	əd	nd	id

Dakuon & Handakuon Katakana flashcards

ギ	グ	ゲ	ゴ
ザ	ジ	ズ	ゼ
ゾ	ダ	ヂ	ヅ
デ	ド	バ	ビ
ブ	ベ	ボ	パ
ピ	プ	ペ	ポ

go	ge	gu	gi
ze	zu	ji	za
du	di	da	zo
bi	ba	do	de
pa	bo	be	bu
po	pe	pu	pi

Made in the USA
Columbia, SC
18 December 2024

50057601R00096